the Sound of Seeds

poetry by Robin Lily Goldberg

The Sound of Seeds

poetry by Robin Lily Goldberg

First printing April, 2014

Front cover photo by Michael Forster Rothbart
www.mfrphoto.com
Back cover photo by Jessica Madeline Goldberg

Published by:
Charing Cross Press
P. O. Box 6052
Ann Arbor, Michigan
48106-6052
Telephone: (734) 971-3455
Email: charingcrosspressbooks@gmail.com

Printed in the United States by
Sheridan Books, Inc., Chelsea, Michigan

ISBN: 978-0-9826320-7-9

Books can be ordered directly from Charing Cross Press at a cost of $11.00.
(If the book is to be mailed, there is an additional $3 charge for postage/handling.)

Acknowledgements

To my parents,
>for introducing me to poetry.

To my younger sister,
>for becoming my role model.

To my grandmothers,
>for always appreciating my writing.

To Kaela and Liz Z.,
>for inspiring me artistically.

To Ken, Jeff, Jennifer and Liz G.,
>for encouraging me academically.

To my Shambhava teachers and fellow trainees,
>for supporting me spiritually.

To Hal,
>for swimming over to introduce himself.

To Gloria, Sara, Carol, Joanna, Paulette, Andrew, Heather, and Leila,
>for joining me on my journey.

To *Spider* magazine,
>for seeing potential in my snowflake.

The poems "Rituals" and "3 Strikes" first appeared
in *The Journal of Modern Poetry*.

The poems "Among Internal Organs," "Green Grammar," and
"I drip from a glass of orange juice" first appeared in
CRAM by Chicago Poetry Press.

The author thanks these publications for recognizing her work.

Author's Introduction

Through music and movement, poetry produced the soundtrack of my childhood. Now I watch in amazement as these forms of expression continue to orchestrate my life in adulthood.

In the midst of a record cold winter, this collection emerged organically, reviving my faith in growth. Each chapter corresponds to a stage of the breath, bridging the mind and body. The poems appear in pairs that speak directly to each other. Then they flow into the following pair, creating a diverse yet cohesive poetry community.

As a writer, I seek to illustrate ideas that resonate with people of all ages and origins. Although I do not expect readers to understand the literal meaning of each word I write, I do believe they can connect with the essence of every poem.

Thank you for opening to this page and to new possibilities with words. As you sense your way through *the Sound of Seeds*, I hope you find yourself in every poem.

— Robin Lily Goldberg, Spring 2014

Table of Contents

Inhaling

Hovering

Exhaling

Resonating

Inhaling

Traveling tea

hibiscus
and licorice
sprawl across an urban meadow

they leap through Olympic rings
and dangle down my arms
like vines of henna

an old-fashioned marquee
points them toward Rome
or Baton Rouge

they catch a ride
in my cupped hands
and call them home

Around the block

I grab an umbrella for my morning walk,
not realizing that it's made of cereal boxes.

A guitar with green chickenpox
plays in the background.

I spot rare crayons
sprouting from broken bottles on the sidewalk.

Bottle caps rain over the nativity
where factoids disappear.

Candle wax drips onto stained glass windows,
repelling water like a quilt.

I melt like a summer record
onto the front steps.

A Waterproof Journal

I start
by sliding lucky dinosaurs out of the sock drawer.
Porcelain giraffes
don't cut it anymore.
I hop into a hot air balloon
and sail to Munich
where I sow the seeds of Stonehenge.
They grow into puzzle pieces
that set the stage
for sandy pages.

Literacy

I read Egyptian myths like labyrinths,
avoiding corners like stale cereal.

I read about dust devils
and rivers beneath the sand.
They trickle down to Cape Town,
        leaving scribbles in damp caves.

I read through magnifying glasses
to see the dome of Notre Dame.
        When the rose window splinters,
        I climb a circular staircase to safety.

I read my route from above,
        noting pottery shards to avoid.
But only Navajo wheels
will lead me away from dead ends.

Nonfiction

Maya Lin paints insects
with Crayolas.

Duke Ellington records
on rollerskates.

Roberto Clemente rides submarines
though Arizona.

Susan B. Anthony
toasts marshmallows.

Tennessee Williams
recites bedtime stories
in French.

Poetic Analysis

Comparing seamstresses to rocks
  requires scissors,
        glue,
        and skill.
We begin by sizing up the Earth
  to find a mask that fits her ears.
  The one with marble strings,
  ties neatly in a bow.
     White roses insulate her hat,
          but she hears fossils of the news.
               Our restless brothers send reports of
               dinosaurs through telegrams.
                    They gallop through her fingers
               to dream upon gold fringe.
          Our ambitious plants grow into gorges,
               and she fills them by the moon.
     She trims the sand
  and weaves our words into a globe.
Comparing seamstresses to rocks
  requires nothing
        but a pen.

Multi-Monologue

she loves her hair
she highlights it with a red headband

her mother fears baldness
she braids baked goods with rhymes

her grandmother repels white leather
she hides with the pipes in the cellar

her aunt loses pennies and finds fortune tellers
she follows them towards names

Rituals

You sip coffee beans
        while I write the paper.

You shower at 8
        and I bathe in orange juice.

You ski to the office
        but I ride my red wagon.

You see through violins,
        I choreograph for horses.

You hum like a mouse
        and I sing in Sanskrit.

You greet gophers
        but I recycle napkins.

You rake the leaves
        while I root for robots.

You take light bulbs to bed,
        I take stained glass windows.

You sleep with long fingernails
        but I play the piano.

You sip cocoa beans
        while I print the paper.

Divination

When soap dishes squirt
into the rabbit's nest,
I soak my heels in archeology.
When spatulas slip out
from within the wagon,
I dry my freckles with a bamboo tissue
as my watch harmonizes in Celsius.
My thermometer measures candle flavors
until tapestries skate westward,
filling jam jars with whiskers.
I scoop bubbles into an envelope,
listening for the smell of sun
knitting spoons into a compass.

Hypotheses

Without a hat I'd be an eagle,
   fearless enough to fly in February.
My father would stop
    to take my photo.
      in black & white.

Without a skirt I'd be a rat,
   scurrying through grimy streets.
My sister would stop traffic
    to let me cross.
      in the city.

Without glasses I'd be a mole,
   inching along the muddy driveway.
My mother would stop the minivan
    to save me.
      in slow motion.

Oxygen

tuesday is the first day (geometrically).
we toast to bones and rubber bands but
I don't. tuesday
comes first, intuitively,
like letters
arriving at union station.
I've hugged each delay until I need
sunless, newborn breaths.
sunless, yet
full of letters made of lines,
not sentences.
the cursive drains,
the calcium drains,
my diamonds will drain out of the clock,
onto the tracks,
where barefeet are waiting.
my alphabet will drain into a face,
full of fingers,
free from squares.

Inhale Letters, Exhale Words

          She teaches enunciation by tossing
yellow beads into his
          mouth.
She fills him with marbles
     that sound like buttons.
If he wakes up,
               he'll swallow one.

The men flaunt their newspapers
          but only one reads
               fine print.
He wears paint on his jeans
and scratches his raw hands
too.

The jeweler highlights with colored pencils.
The boy absorbs words through a pillow.
The painter peruses the scores.
The "man" reads textbooks for romance.

When the paperboys leave,
she nods off
               while he sleeps,
                    with lips parted.
     They hear buttons alternate with breaths.

Recipe for Human Rights

1 tree house

2 Spanish dictionaries

a handful of literacy

1 job application

2 cloves of contraception

a pinch of baseball

1 carpool

2 nametags

3 Indonesian songs

Curls

I climbed a hill
and curled a corner,
> listening to Southern drawls
> and love songs.

I rang the doorbell
without an address,
> and slid into a rocking chair.

Leaning against dragon pillows,
I crossed
and uncrossed
> my corduroys.

Avoiding tails
with my teeth,
> I sank into an Eastern meadow.

Content among the moons,
I brushed my hair with branches,
> and fell asleep in the frizz.

Prairie Grass

Rusted tablets
top southern igloos,
curdling at the edges.
Writing utensils wear away inside,
beneath rulers,
wax,
and ribbons.

He counts elephants on an abacus,
stitching foxglove nectar,
leaving tornadoes in denial.

They iron rugs on the trellis
in acrylics
and
send stampless Christmas cards.

I carve pillows on the vines,
gluing Sundays to crayons
and buttons to Brahms,
without washing off the chimney.

Seeds

I uproot Argentina
        to repot in Washington.
My Fridays become weekdays
        without maté.

I shrivel back into a ballerina
        dancing to 4-beat measures.
Suburbia becomes corn country.

I shove bilingualism
        into mismatched shoes.
Blizzards bury harp strings
        beneath Jell-O salad.

I sacrifice bike rides
        for organic galoshes.
The Capitol crosses the country.

I inhale the words
        of invisible neighbors.
Dandelions sprout in the rain.

Hovering

Green Grammar

A sip of chlorophyll
      starts my search
      for Spanish
      in pure form.

no proper nouns.

      Hats hover
            over
            crinkled earth.

no buried lisps,
no mangled roots.

      Free sprinklers
            of sangria
                  pave my way to the museum.

no pompous twang,
no stubby stems.

      Tomatoes hang
            like tapestries.

      I pluck the one
            that sprouts sideways
            and claim it
            as my enyay.

no double yous
      or single whys.

Paperwork

The "R" was for Richie.
    Well-rounded,
    open-minded.
        Grounded by 1 mediocre grade —   not 2.
            A confidant non-consonant,
            sheltered by a camel.
Safe for pink or blue bonnets.
    Tucked snugly between the top 10
    and the immigrants.
        Ready to tell a joke,
        report the news,
        or fly.

Anticipation

The elevator lifts me
        from then
        to now,

        from exhaust
        to incense,

        from pollen
        to sunflower seeds.

Bamboo grass
grows along the curb.

Ancient ivy
winds around the window.

I peer through the leaves,
        fearing the floor
        more than the street.

Impatience

I want to build a bridge
       with fortune-telling popsicle sticks

I want to wake up
       to oatmeal resting on a handmade table

I want to vote
       for females from the past who speak Sign Language

I want to bask beneath Presidential Palm Trees
       with biracial leaves

I want to grow
       organic onions that don't trigger tears

I want to dance through a field
       free from multiple choice bubbles

Chameleons

Snow sticks on sand.

March 29th Album

I.   A yellow bus pulls up
to a log cabin
  and white gloves spill out the door.
    My feet sink
through the jungle carpet.
I smell creamed corn and cat litter,
  decorated with dog leashes.
Stuffed animals sleep on '95 phonebooks.
  Postcards awake them
  with reminders to visit the vet.

II.   A November toboggan
    slides from the rafters,
      dragging family photos over wet leaves.
I hike down the staircase
to uproot ceramics.
    They've cracked
beneath paint cans of snow.

III.   I dodge camouflage helmets
and unloved high-chairs.
Broken branches
    scratch my ears
     as they fall from fake Christmas trees.
Grandpa buries me under dry needles.
  He stares from the fireplace
  without blinking.

Tortoise-shell Sight

The woman who makes wildflowers
grows cows in her minivan.

She hums with the radio-
   whistling is offensive.

On runny days
she rockclimbs
and feeds taxes to the caribou.

She laughs at tortoise-shells-
   not comedies.

Her harp rests on her hip
and molds her fingers to the song.

To fill the generation gap,
   she sleeps with nicknames.

Foreshadowed?

Cursive letters
      spilled
            onto my certificate
      like juicy worms raining down in April.
As they soaked my skin,
      I blossomed from a
            bald baby into a
                  bell between the mountains.
My scent soared to the peaks
      and I followed on pigeon wings.
Flight gave me everything
                  except the blue jay's song.

Morning

Her threads,
   run into
blue threads,
   run into sandstone.

the southwest sleeps actively.

His cheeks dissolve
into the palms
of mothers in profile.

They see brushes,
              birds
                 and lanes,
through a lensless eye.

His hair hangs like a waterfall,
and hers hovers
              like the sky.
Stars peak between the strands
above a sliver of the moon.

Snow feathers
        sing aloud,
defying orange graves.

but within the woven hours,
     his rippled brim
   conceals a sunrise.

Spilling into Sunday

My tree pose tipped
       like a cup of tea,
my pants flooded the bedroom.

We spotted a bride
       along the brick road,
arcing our names through the sky.

A silken astronomer
       served us lunch,
on top of a hot air balloon.

My bathrobe blossomed
       into a gown,
dancing toward natural light.

sipping oxymorons

she cannot brew
     corners,
he cannot breathe
     without
     crushing the harvest,
they cannot grow
     from the same picket fence
     into the same eastern mural,
but I can sip oxymorons.

I drip from a glass of orange juice

I drip from a glass of orange juice
      and seep into earthy cracks of Africa.
I learn new words in English,
    new songs in Chuka.

Our conductor frees his hair from
    cowboy hats
    and gallops
        eastward, wearing plaid.

    He fills our coffee filters

    and I rock one in my arms,
playing bluegrass with its folds.

We roll into primary colors
    where I paint with leafy green.

    We call each other by initials
    and know ourselves by flags.

circulating

yoga poses
fill the evergreen forest
with the scent of yellow pollen
sending echoes through the sand
like young waves
earning air bubbles
to sail eastward

Inversions

A mountain alights on my chest,
      rising like a moon,
      falling like a leaf.

I pull my hair
above the grass
      as if
         spring follows fall.

      Freckles dance
      across my frozen elbows.

      They linger
         until rain
         slides them toward my wrists.

Air flows through my veins
      as if
planes have never been invented.

      I turn left,
      resting my right cheek
      upon the neighbor's lawn.

One eye follows
      as if
         sunlight never melts,
while two eyes stride
      into the snow.

Quarters

The mailbox meets my
future before my past,
with royal visitors
        in between.

The elevator lifts my lashes
        while leaving
my legs behind.

Only
intangible images
rise
with third person sensations.

The hills on her hands
roll like dunes,
calling her home
        to sticky fingers
        and sandy hair.

The heater hums
        her to sleep,
        rocking her shell with the river.

Mendota

for Phyllis

Feathers wave
from the
front window

Popcorn speckles
slate stones
leading toward the door

A single step
launches dandelion dandruff
across the ranch

Breadcrumbs settle
onto the
lingonberry tablecloth

Freckles fall asleep
upon the loft
of the log cabin

Exhaling

Welcome Mat

My host mother
      raises the radio,
      advertising New York brownstones
            in Buenos Aires.

I smother my ears
      with headphones
      and jog over eggshells toward the beach.

Yolks glisten
      in a nest of baby wrinkles,
         warmed by my glowing pants.

I eye them like an archeologist,
I poke them like a veterinarian.

I don't need a job,
      but I do need a turtle,

      and a place to wipe my feet.

The Newbie

Your southern bob distains me—
so I'll ignore you.
I don't need your business cards because I won an Oscar and
    I have connections (to the sandwich-maker).
I know where to find 1969 prices,
and I can sustain myself on animation and vintage tops.
"Yeah, I crochet,"
    but you don't seem to notice that I'm not a golfer.
I'm a carpooling professor
    and "I'm very social."
        I love lawsuits but ferns can kill me,
    so don't sell me any seeds.
I came because my curtainrod is falling,
    but all you can offer me is a coupon for a corsage.
"Thanks"-but my samples have run out.

Circular Squares

I begin backwards,
a feminist
following the leader
through the forest

I bake the bread
and drop the crumbs
yet let grapevines
grow around my limbs

My underarms tell fairytales
but my elbows
tell the truth

I listen to geometry
and swing into the trees

But when branches
catch and cradle me,
my skirts become my sphere

Square Subtitles

lie down-
on the flag-shaped pillow.
it flies the same
in Alaska and Asia.
the city saddens the country,
and everyone gets wet.

dry off-
with red newspapers.
songs come from
heads resting on calligraphy.

speak up-
for painted faces.
forget the lyrics,
remember the colors.
sleep out loud.

Minnesota

Hoop skirts and pigtails with cousins who "should" be doing nothing or studying Scriptures because she never wears a coat when it's over 20 degrees and is used to the smokehouse which is how you get to cook for the governor even though you work in construction and get into the Air Force fitting lime Swedish Fish sardines into a can with a cardboard lid while doing a Rubik's cube of Sudoku in under 2 minutes which you lose when competing against another physics major (and what did he major in?) because he travels all over the country and the world working but doing I don't know what besides rock climbing and skiing just like the other son from the divorced family but I guess it doesn't matter as long as he loves it.

Warren Dunes

the marsh dries up
into late November leaves,
veins crumble into grains of sand
that fill our shoes

the bowl cannot catch
the strawberry jelly that oozes out
of Swedish Danishes

we wash our hands with milk,
dry them on the beach,
logroll down the dunes

glaze drowns out the alewives,
glues our fingers to our lips

the breeze scoops homes
for our barefeet
in freshwater spoons

3 Strikes

Rice was the safest sustenance
until hips, lips, and hair
sealed the envelope.

The stamp sailed from China
to Chechnya
on a boat propelled
by magazines and cigarettes.

They planted the seeds in a baseball field,
beneath headscarves,
and fed them fertilizer.

Not even tornadoes
could have whipped the West,
South and Northeast
into shape so quickly.

Think Twice

Kansas City sits in Missouri.

The Venus flytrap grows on Earth.

French fries started in Spain.

Chicken fingers come from breasts.

Instant oatmeal cooks in 60 seconds.

Seedless watermelon has seeds.

Hamburgers contain beef.

Cowboys ride horses.

Humans wear pony tails.

Perms last temporarily.

Glasses have plastic lenses.

Eyelashes feel soft.

Stoplights say when to go.

Public bathrooms don't have tubs.

Soap opera stars don't sing.

Two Shades of Green

Laundromats cost more than movie theaters,
so I wash my socks in the sink.

    Lake Michigan grows.

The price of meat skyrockets,
so I become a vegetarian.

    The endangered species list shrinks.

Notebook paper is too expensive,
so I write on my leather pants.

    Rainforests sprout upwards.

I can't afford a car,
so I inflate bicycle tires like balloons.

    My carbon footprint walks backwards.

Red Reasons

a hidden hand
reveals a dozen reasons

to return
to the familiar room
of foreign flavors

to read
about the little redhead
from the funny pages

to roll
beneath a blanket
of snow

and never question hands again

saturation

beside the baby powder sky blue kiddie pool,
i wring out
thumbelina's viscous epic
in my mother's _____ (grade school) voice.
From the clothesline, I feel wrinkles dripping.
From the trellis, I hear pollen gossiping.
From the swings, I see
a strawberry tiara
launching from a plié
into the dimples of a sponge.

Polvo

A dusty rabbit lives outside my bedroom door.
He follows me to the keyboard
where I type 3 months worth of words
to read on a rainy day.

When I reach for the last loaf,
I find an empty cage.
My hair no longer wraps itself around my waist
where it belongs.

I confuse Christmas colors
and fly to the airport by accident.
Grandma helps me cross the highway
where I wait for the dustbowl to subside.

I enter through the archway
30 minutes past the bell.
Gnomes surround my tri-colored lips
yet mix-up "none" and "neither."

Back home I let the water run too long.
Then I score 50% on my fruit salad.
But with another rabbit,
my dust will dissolve into words.

Confession

white aprons
shroud
stomachs and sneakers

miscarried sisters
obscure
thin ice

pure milk
conceals
poison

Among Internal Organs

I apologize for planting your pens
in the sink.
For rinsing them with roosters
and drenching the feathers.

I'm sorry for calling you a toaster.
For stuffing salt in your pockets
and pacing chess tiles
to make you "ping!"

I apologize for painting your song
on the sole of my shoe.
For squelching your lyrics
on my way to the laundromat.

I'm sorry for selling your name to the mailman.
For sending geese to your door.
For flying home
on the flaps.

Medicine

Just because I'm not an obstetrician
     in India
     doesn't mean
          I'm not worth 1 signature.

I'm going to Java
to play the peking
     4 times faster
     than a fetal heart monitor.
I'll play the last 2 notes backwards and

still

     save the world
     from AIDS and poverty.

Just because C-sections sound Western
     doesn't mean I have to
     turn my drum
          into a rain barrel.

When the surgeon gets sick
     I'll play without gloves.
My songs will deliver

more

     than healthy babies.

Exhalation

for Helen

We landed
on our palms,
seeking sisters

We sang
of sweets,
and authenticity

We sprinkled
sacred soil,
and cradled our stones

Resonating

Tall days

I looked for colonial hats
    and found bald spots.
sprouting from wooden benches.

We made a sphere
      of human antennas
and rotated like words.

I listened for Sanskrit chants
    and heard silence.
broken by birds becoming airplanes.

I saw the minute hand
     spin forward
and we parted with "good morning"

Treehouse Notes

I awake to a marimba
floating over flying buttresses.
I follow the sound
through a yellow door
into a birdhouse
of affable squirrels.
We listen to a summer camp broadcast
and they teach me
the Alaskan Lobster Trap Maneuver.
Then the leaves crinkle,
  the telescope dims,
and the equinox falls asleep.

my notebook

whistles
      ride the rhine
      through the wine
          lands
   to greet a grassy
dream sequence
      over the pier

july jingle bells
      gurgle like snow white's
         curls
as she chimes the triangle
     followed by a xylophone

tin can tunes
      ooze through their lips
as they bounce banjos
     on their knees
       like baby barcelonas

Weathered scrolls

Scales
slide down
deerskin walls,
glossing over
feathered duck fabric
on their way
to visit
the vegan widower

A missionary
washes woolen bracelets
among a herd of cows

Bells
bring their robes
to the shoemaker
without
shearing their stems first

And a musician
sleeps beneath rags
woven by rain

White prints

Follow the birdseed trail
      and the sound of my swingset
         to the backdoor
            of the trees.

   snap on your toes

     to keep track of the tune.

  Spell your name in the snow,
    glide over beeswax,
      and look for the lonely mosquito.

  If you slide with a rooster
  and choose stubborn curves,
  you'll ride among cotton vines.

Follow night branches
     to a loop of green lace.

   listen, deer.

    hear your name in the snow.

Pink versus Red

One cat waves
and writes me a rhyming poem
on a cherry blossom.

Another widens
his marble eyes
and eats my chocolate rose.

My sister's mutt
sleeps in my purse
and steals my lipstick.

The third cat retrieves it
and prances across the keys,
hitting the ninth note of every octave.

Painting

Allegro
sprinkles horizontally
       from her parasol
       to her canopy
       to her kettle of Zinnia,
   filled in 1947.

Chromatic Autobiography

age three.
I rocked in a cradle,
humming with geese,
swaying with sheep.

age seven.
I sat in the school auditorium,
sipping a recorder,
digesting a clarinet.

age twelve.
I peddled my brother's bike,
tossing newspapers,
reading sheet music.

age twenty.
I lived in a tree,
composing with bark,
swaying with pigeons.

age fifty.
I cooked in a closet,
hanging chords,
stacking signatures.

age eighty.
I rock in my chair,
recalling recorders,
painting colorless dots.

Triplets

Irene Castle waltzes through streamers
dangling from the chandelier

90 chocolate kisses frame the floor
and she steals one as she swoops by

Roses hover from her ears
in a pose with Audrey Hepburn

Their scent fades when a $90 roast
takes center stage

She sings Venetian sailor songs
with Mary Tyler Moore

Her curls bounce like bunny ears
as she skates to annual tunes

When 90 candles melt the ice
she glides back beneath the streamers

She seals her steps in envelopes
with cards to read next year

Rehearsing Underwater

dragons reverberate
through the river

        strands of silver
        stream through the microphone

                whispers rise through organ pipes,
                drifting toward the moon.

                        weave headscarves
                        through the keyboard

                  play flower pots
                  like handbells

collect minor keys,
in copper bowls.

Kecak

Two monkey chants
       turn our fingers
              into fall colors.

Maples
squat like hedgehogs

     in syncopated patterns.

Through coffee,
       tea,
       and cream
we paddle toward tourists,

            docking at our doorbells.

One human gong
      dims the coals
           for the night.

Nomadic Masterpieces

A leopard swings in the moonlight,
      spots waltzing along a branch.
He stops at a fountain in London
      to toss in a castanet.

A gondolier calls to clothespins,
      ribbons rising up a scale.
He stops at a fountain in Venice
      to toss in a violin.

They inhale nocturnal air
      and exhale wordless songs.
They stop at fountains in Boston
      to toss out old inventions.

Recipe in C

start with steam rising
     like a ringing gong

bob your knee
     to the beat of hollow drumsticks

smell whole notes simmering
     like cymbals

salt the stew
     with Australian accents

cook the islands until tender

Echo

The lake is lined with faces
that never call my name.
They think I'm from a fairy tale,
but I'm real,
and I'd come running.
If they called.

Photosynthesis

An automatic flash
fills our eyes
      with personal panoramas

Foreign words
fill our ears
      with eastern promises

We paint our plans
      and print our names

We sing with organic accents
      in unfamiliar fields

We write with road maps
      and sign in calligraphy

From black-and-white
      to rising blue,

our Polaroid
      becomes the winning photo

the Sound of Seeds

We rise with lemons
            waking from the wood,
and roll onto a humming rug

Breathing with our namesakes

We rise toward a reason to inhale,
and dive toward a reason to exhale

Rolling our vertebrae into aspens

We hear the bell between the pines,
and smell the citrus sun

Breathing with strangers

We rise to the tune of today,
and roll to the rhythm of waves

Hearing the chimes
            above the drums

About the Author

Robin Lily Goldberg grew up in River Forest, Illinois and now lives in Ann Arbor, Michigan. Since publishing her first poem in *Spider* magazine at age six, she has studied creative writing at Kenyon College and the University of Michigan. When not writing, she teaches yoga and contributes to a storytelling program for hospital patients.